Text copyright © 2018 by Isabel Thomas
Cover art and interior illustrations copyright © 2018 by Alex Paterson
Additional images courtesy of Shutterstock

Random House and the colophon are registered trademarks
of Penguin Random House LLC.

Visit us on the Web! rhcbooks.com

Educators and librarians, for a variety of teaching tools, visit us at RHTeachersLibrarians.com

Library of Congress Cataloging-in-Publication Data is available upon request.
ISBN 978-0-593-30867-7 (hardcover) | ISBN 978-0-593-30868-4 (lib. bdg.) |
ISBN 978-0-593-30869-1 (ebook)

Printed in Canada
10 9 8 7 6 5 4 3 2 1
First American Edition

THIS BOOK IS NOT GARBAGE

50 WAYS TO DITCH PLASTIC, REDUCE TRASH, AND SAVE THE WORLD!

ISABEL THOMAS
ILLUSTRATED BY ALEX PATERSON

RANDOM HOUSE  NEW YORK

CONTENTS

QUICK GUIDE TO THE

PLANET-O-METER

SAVES:

WILDLIFE   PAPER/WOOD   ELECTRICITY   LITTER/LANDFILL

PLASTIC   RAIN FOREST   RECYCLING   CARBON FOOTPRINT

POLLUTION   WATER   FOOD

IMPACT: COST: DIFFICULTY:

LIVING ON THE VEG!

When it comes to gobbling up resources, meaty meals are the planet's number one enemy. Going veggie for one day each week can make a BIG difference.

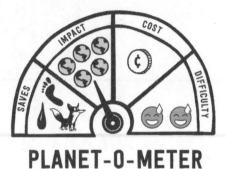

PLANET-O-METER

Every year, 7.6 billion humans chomp their way through meat from an amazing 65 billion animals. Raising these animals—and getting them from the farm to your burger bun—puts pressure on the planet in three ways.

HELP!

BAA BAA LAND

Most of the world's farmland—and almost one-third of all usable land—is devoted to raising animals for meat and milk. It's not just fields of grass playing home to cows and sheep: almost a third of the crops we grow are used to feed animals, too. This farmland has replaced forests and destroyed natural habitats.

FEROCIOUS FARTS

Greenhouse gases trap heat in the atmosphere, causing global warming. Livestock emit the same amount of greenhouse gases as all the fossil fuel–guzzling vehicles in the world! Cows are the **WORST** culprits.

As they digest grass, they constantly burp and fart methane, one of the most harmful greenhouse gases. Each of the 1.5 billion cattle on the planet can expel up to 132 gallons of methane in a day!

WATER WORRIES

Looking after all those animals accounts for nearly 10 percent of all the fresh water that humans use each year. Even more water is used to keep meat clean and cool on its journey from field to fork. Animal farming is also one of the main sources of water pollution, because animal poop and chemicals wash into rivers and oceans.

Scientists have crunched the numbers and calculated the carbon footprints of some favorite meaty meals:

Half a leg of lamb

86 pounds of carbon dioxide, or **93 miles** in an average car

Four large beef burgers

59.5 pounds of carbon dioxide, or **65 miles** in an average car

20 pork sausages

26.7 pounds of carbon dioxide, or **31 miles** in an average car

If you and your family avoid meat (and cheese, too) for just one day a week, it could help the planet more than taking your family car off the road for **4.5 WEEKS.**

What about the other six days? Well, if you love meat too much to go veggie but you want to be kinder to the environment, stick with chicken, and fish that's caught in a responsible way. Eggs are an even greener source of animal protein (but DON'T eat them if they actually are green).

By 2050, at least 9 BILLION people will be sharing our planet. (Fifty years ago there were just 3.5 billion.) It's not possible for all those people to feast on beef and lamb. Protein will HAVE to come from different sources. Some of the ideas scientists are working on include "cultured meat" grown in labs, and protein from insects! That bean burger's starting to look pretty good now, isn't it?!

DITCH THE DISHES

You hate it, and the planet hates it too! Happily, putting less effort into doing the dishes is a win-win situation.

PLANET-O-METER

Have you ever considered taking part in some scientific research? Scientists are always looking for people to help test their theories. **BUT BE CAREFUL WHAT YOU VOLUNTEER FOR**. The unlucky participants in one scientific study were asked to wash 144 dirty dishes, pots, pans, and utensils—**EACH**! It did have a purpose, though. The study found that people approached the task in very different ways—some much kinder to the environment than others.

Washing the dishes uses about 5 percent of **ALL** water we use at home. A typical household washes dishes by hand 10 times a week, using **7.9 GALLONS** of water if the washing or rinsing is done under a running tap. It's possible to use much less if you avoid wasteful habits like running hot water to rinse dishes. Every minute, a running faucet pours out 2 to 3 gallons of water—a week's worth of drinking water.

Heating this water releases the equivalent of **17.6 pounds** of carbon dioxide—that's as much as if you left a 42-inch LCD TV on for **48 hours**.

COUNTDOWN TO ECO-FRIENDLY DISHWASHING

5. Scrape as much leftover food as possible into your compost container (see pages 62–65).

4. Fill the sink with warm (not hot) water—and only when you have a full load of dishes to wash.

3. Wash glasses and utensils first. Then wash dirtier dishes. Pile the soapy dishes up on the dish drainer.

2. Fill the sink halfway with cold water. Dip the soapy dishes in for a rinse.

1. Leave the dishes to air-dry.

If your family uses a dishwasher, you'll be **VERY** pleased to hear they can be kinder to the planet—as long as you don't rinse the dishes first. A typical dishwasher cycle only uses 3.2 to 4 gallons of water, but prerinsing dishes under the faucet can waste a shocking 5,812 gallons of water each year! Instead, scrape any leftovers into your compost container (see pages 62–65). Some modern smart dishwashers can sense how dirty dishes are, and adjust their settings accordingly.

For extra eco-points, always make sure the dishwasher is completely full, use the coolest cycle possible, and run the dishwasher in the middle of the night to make the most of greener electricity (see pages 81–83). Save the planet while you sleep (and don't ruin your good work by arguing about whose turn it is to unload!).

Did you know that drying the dishes is bad for you? No, not just because it's boring! In one scientific study, 89 percent of kitchen towels harbored bacteria from poop. BLERGH. In a quarter of the cases, this included *E. coli* bacteria, which can cause nasty stomach bugs. Throw in the (kitchen) towel, and save water and energy on laundry, too.

A BAN ON BATHS!

Want to know why the bathroom is a battleground for eco-warriors?

PLANET-O-METER

One of the top ways to cut the volume of greenhouse gases belched into the air by our houses is to reduce the amount of water we heat up at home. In Japan, for example, supplying and heating water for homes causes 5 percent of all carbon dioxide emissions, and 60 percent of this hot water is used for bathing. Skipping even one bath each week can make a **BIG** difference. Swap it for a short shower so you don't get too stinky.

If you already prefer showers, don't be too smug. Fast-flowing and rainfall showerheads use up to 4.5 gallons of water per minute, meaning that an average eight-minute shower can use almost double the energy and water of a bath!

To make showers more eco-friendly, time yourself and get out after five minutes. Use a waterproof watch or a windup egg timer. (NEVER use devices that plug in to the wall in the shower.) Encourage your family to take the five-minute shower challenge too, and you could save hundreds of gallons of hot water—and hundreds of dollars—every year.

Banning baths and taking speedy showers aren't the only ways to save water in the bathroom. You can be an eco-warrior every time you use the sink or toilet. Brushing your teeth for two minutes uses about 3 gallons of water each time (that's 6 gallons per day if you brush twice a day—which you do, don't you?!). If you turn the faucet off while brushing, you'll save a lot of water. If you usually run the faucet while you wash your face or hands, fill the sink partway instead and save an extra 3.2 gallons!

TURN THE TAP OFF!

Each person in the United States uses an average of 80 to 100 gallons of clean water every day. Across the US, more than 1 trillion gallons is used on showers alone.

TURN BOTTLES INTO BOOMERANGS

If you haven't heard how bad plastic water bottles are by now, you've been living on a different planet . . . one that's not being choked by a giant floating garbage patch.

More than 480 **BILLION** plastic bottles are sold around the world every year, adding up to a planet-sized problem. Placed end to end, these bottles would circle the world about 1,870 times . . . and that's almost exactly what's happening. Each year, millions of tons of plastic litter reaches the oceans, where this trash collects in gigantic floating garbage patches.

PLANET-O-METER

Plastic's greatest strength—being almost indestructible—is also its greatest problem. While paper and cardboard rot away in weeks, plastic bottles take at least **450 YEARS** to wear down. And even then, plastic doesn't decompose completely—it just breaks into smaller and smaller pieces. The United Nations has warned that these tiny pieces, called microplastics, are doing irreparable damage to the creatures that live in seas and oceans.

In the minute it took you to read this far, **1 MILLION** plastic bottles were bought, beginning a journey that all too often ends in the stomachs of zooplankton, fish, albatross chicks, whales, and seals.

Whether you're puffing and panting on the playing field, sweating through the school dance, or crying tears of boredom in a grammar lesson, you need to drink all day long to replace the water your body uses. But this doesn't have to come from a disposable plastic bottle. After all, PET (the plastic used for most soft drink and water bottles) wasn't invented until the 1970s, and at least 100 billion people had managed not to die of dehydration before then! Plastic is a bad habit, and it's up to us all to break it.

So, what can you do? Here are some ideas. Invest in a bottle that's easy to clean and reuse. Write your name on it so it comes back to you, like a boomerang! Fill it up before you go out for the day, and while you're on the move, look for water fountains or ask at a café or restaurant if you can get a refill. And if you find yourself filling up your water bottle in a coffee shop while the adults around you clutch disposable coffee cups with disposable plastic lids, be sure to bring out your best hard stare.

About 120 billion coffee cups are used and thrown away each year in the United States.

If you do end up with a disposable plastic bottle, it's not the end of the world (well, not yet)—make sure you reuse it as many times as possible before finding a recycling bin. Keep an eye out for deposit bottles, too—in some states you can even make money by collecting discarded bottles and taking them to be recycled.

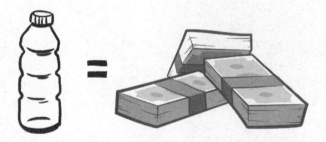

Since plastic was invented in the early 1900s, about 8.3 billion tons has been produced . . . and about 6.3 billion tons of this has been thrown away. Only 9 percent has been recycled. The rest is sitting in landfills or elsewhere in the environment, quietly not rotting away. If we don't want a plastic planet, we need to take action now.

According to one study, by 2050 the plastic in the world's oceans will weigh more than all the fish.

PARTY FOR THE PLANET

Each birthday is a celebration that you've made one more trip around the sun . . . so why not plan a party to look after the planet that gave you a ride?

PLANET-O-METER

Parties are awesome, but for the planet they're no cause for celebration. Birthdays come only once a year, so most party goods are disposable. Wrapping paper, cards, decorations, paper plates and napkins, and plastic cups and utensils are designed to be used for a few hours and then thrown away. But it doesn't have to be this way.

COUNTDOWN TO AN ECO-FRIENDLY PARTY

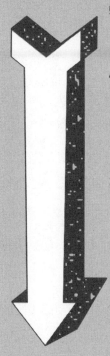

5. Send your invitations and thank-you cards by email.

4. Make your own banner by sticking triangles of used wrapping paper, comics, or scrap fabric to a piece of string or raffia.

3. Use washable plates, cups, and utensils to serve food and drinks. You might be able to pick up a whole set secondhand for less than the price of disposables! Keep them in a special box between parties and lend them to friends and family, too.

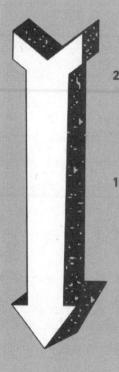

2. No napkins! Provide a bowl of soapy water and a towel instead. Set out small compost and recycling bins to make sure garbage ends up in the right place.

1. Instead of filling plastic party bags with plastic toys, get your guests to make a gift to take home. How about decorating a clay plant pot, sciencing up some slime, or creating your own cupcakes?

Americans are some of the biggest fans of plastic knives, forks, and spoons, using an estimated 40 billion per year. The European Union has already passed a law banning single-use plastic plates and eating utensils, beginning in 2021.

DUMP THE GLITTER

Glitter—so shiny, so sparkly, so pretty . . . AND SO DEADLY!

PLANET-O-METER

Glitter is made out of tiny pieces of reflective foil coated with colored plastic. Used in items from clothes to cosmetics to craft kits, glitter has never been more popular. But for eco-heroes, it's definitely lost its sparkle.

Anyone who's used glitter knows that the tiny flakes get **EVERYWHERE**. Receive one sparkly card, and you're washing it out of your hair, carpet, and dog for weeks. But have you thought about where the glitter goes once you wash it down the drain? Straight through water-filtration systems and into the oceans, where it can do terrible damage to the creatures that live there (see page 134).

These tiny plastic particles also make their way back to our plates.
Hundreds of marine animals eat plastic. (In the ocean, plastic particles
quickly become covered with a layer of algae, which makes them
smell delicious to fish.) So every time we eat fish or seafood, we're
also eating microplastics or the chemicals that have leaked out of
them. Being a vegetarian doesn't help, either—plastic fibers have
been found in sea salt and even in honey. No one knows yet what the
impact on human health will be. Glitter doesn't seem so pretty now,
does it?

But there is a glimmer of light at the end of the tunnel. Scientists are
researching biodegradable glitter made from natural materials such
as eucalyptus instead of plastic. So if you can't resist a bit of sparkle
in your face paint, bath bombs, or craft supplies, try to track down
this eco-glitter. Or you could follow the lead of one day care group
in England and try using lentils instead (although maybe not on your
face . . .).

Scientists think that 15 TRILLION to
51 TRILLION microplastic particles have
already made their way into the oceans.

EAT UGLY FOOD

Be an eco-superhero in the supermarket by playing the ugly-food game. Who can track down (and take home) the strangest-looking fruits and veggies?

PLANET-O-METER

Time to get (even more) serious for a minute: 815 million people—one in ten of the world's population—don't have enough to eat, and undernutrition causes the deaths of more than 3 million children every year. But the problem is not that the planet can't produce enough food to feed everyone. Shockingly, a **THIRD** of the food produced every year gets thrown away.

Time to GET SERIOUS.

The waste happens in many different places—on farms, where crops that don't look perfect are left to rot; in supermarkets, where "ugly" fruit and vegetables aren't displayed or are left on the shelves by shoppers; and in our homes, where food is forgotten at the back of the fridge until it's too spoiled to eat. In the United States, about 14 percent of all garbage sent to landfills is food that has been thrown away.

Our shopping, cooking, and eating habits are a big part of the problem. This means we have the power to be part of the solution, too! Each time you help with grocery shopping, make it your mission to find the ugliest fruits and vegetables you can. No item is too blemished, big, small, or gnarly—if it's on the shelf, it's safe to eat. Give ugly produce a home so it isn't thrown away—it will still taste delicious!

When we waste food, we waste all the energy it takes to grow, harvest, transport, and package it, too. And if food goes to the landfill and rots, it produces methane, a greenhouse gas. In the United States, the average household wastes almost one-third of the food that comes into the home. In all, this food waste is responsible for about 3.3 gigatons of greenhouse gas emissions every year. That is greater than the TOTAL greenhouse gases of every country in the world except for the United States and China!

SNACK TO SAVE THE WORLD

Billions of people who are lucky enough to live in houses with electricity may take it for granted: it's invisible and just a flick of a switch away, so we don't think about how much we use.

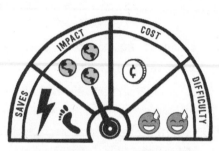

PLANET-O-METER

It's easy to forget where electricity comes from. After all, tablets and TVs don't belch smoke and soot. But the dirty truth is that most of the energy used to generate electricity still comes from burning fossil fuel—an eco-warrior's archenemy.

Burning coal, oil, or natural gas releases huge volumes of gases such as carbon dioxide, which increase the natural greenhouse effect of Earth's atmosphere. The result? A planet that's heating up, leading to long-term climate change. The bad news is that this will cause a rise in sea levels, severe flooding, extreme weather, drought, extinction of many species, food shortages, and the spread of diseases. Unfortunately, there is no good news about burning fossil fuels.

Governments and the energy industry are exploring alternative energy sources, but in the meantime we can all help by trying to use less electricity.

TOP FIVE ECO-TIPS FOR ZAPPING YOUR ELECTRICITY USE

5 Open your curtains or blinds first thing in the morning instead of reaching for the light switch. Turn lights off when you leave a room (unless someone else is in it, of course!).

4 Don't leave the fridge door open too long while you forage for a snack. Up to 7 percent of the appliance's total energy use goes to cooling the warm air that rushes in when the door is opened.

SNACK TIME!

3 Fridges use less energy if they are no more than two-thirds full. If your fridge is overcrowded, start munching to save the planet!

2 When you use devices with screens, turn the volume off and the brightness down so they need charging less often.

1 Don't leave TVs, computers, and consoles on standby overnight. The lazy way to do this is to plug them into a timer device, which will do the remembering for you.

TURN TRASH
INTO TREASURE

Do you ever dream of finding buried treasure and making your fortune? Try digging in your recycling bin!

PLANET-O-METER

It might look like garbage and smell like garbage, but to someone else, it's just what they were looking for. Many people, from artists to teachers, need household materials to use in craft projects. Go on a scavenger hunt for the following items:

- ☆ toilet paper and paper towel rolls
- ☆ egg cartons
- ☆ empty glass jars and perfume bottles
- ☆ old buttons
- ☆ bent coat hangers
- ☆ scraps of fabric
- ☆ pine cones
- ☆ corks from bottles

- ☆ ring pulls from cans
- ☆ plastic milk bottle caps
- ☆ metal bottle caps

Once you've built up a collection, ask your parents to sell it for you online using a "pre-loved" or auction site. Your junk will be less likely to end up in a landfill and could even be turned into something beautiful. To go the extra mile for the environment, donate the proceeds to your favorite eco charity, or use it to "adopt" an endangered animal.

BE SURE TO FOLLOW THESE RULES:

Only collect clean, safe items in good condition.

Ask an adult to do the selling and sending for you. Don't use online selling websites yourself.

Collect used packaging material; then reuse it to pack up and send your items.

PLAN A TRASHY DAY OUT...

... and find out where your garbage goes.

PLANET-O-METER

Imagine if your family stopped putting the garbage out and stored all your trash at home instead. It would soon get pretty stinky. Think the smelliest cheese, mixed with rotten eggs and your sneakers after a game (okay, maybe not **THAT** bad). After a year, you'd be wading through THREE-QUARTERS OF A TON of packaging and food waste for each person in your household.

Most of us are super lucky that our garbage gets taken away every week, but it means we never get to see how much waste we really produce. While you can't start stockpiling it in your bedroom, you can do the next best thing. Find out where your trash goes once you've waved goodbye to the garbage truck.

HAPPY BIRTHDAY, ~~ME~~ PLANET

**Next time you're writing
your birthday wish list,
include a present
for the planet, too!**

PLANET-O-METER

People **LOVE** to give presents—even more than they like receiving
them! (Okay, there are exceptions. . . .) You can go anywhere in the
world and find people giving gifts to strengthen bonds with family
and friends. Scientists who study gift-giving (surely one of the most
awesome jobs on the planet #jobgoals) have found that the perfect
gift is not the most expensive one—it's a gift that someone has
actually asked for. So let's start asking for stuff that has the power to
save the planet!

*The **PERFECT GIFT** is
something that someone
has actually asked for!*

Many landfill and recycling sites offer free tours for individuals or groups. If your family isn't up for it, ask your teacher to organize a class trip. You'll learn what happens to waste in your area, and wha[t] steps you can take to reduce the amount you throw away. You mig[ht] even see high-tech garbage robots sorting materials and making bales. And once you've seen the scale of a stinky landfill site, you['ll] **DEFINITELY** be inspired to reduce, reuse, and recycle like never b[efore]. Plus your bedroom will look **REALLY** clean in comparison!

Instead of more "stuff," ask for activities or planet-friendly gifts like these:

BIRTHDAY WISH LIST

* Movie tickets.
* A special day out with a family member.
* Ask the gift giver to "adopt" an endangered animal on your behalf.
* Let friends and family know that you're happy to receive pre-loved gifts, such as a great piece of clothing or a book that they've read and enjoyed.
* Or ask for a gift card that you can spend on something you really need, rather than a present that might go to waste.

There's always that one relative who will ignore your birthday wish list and get you a book that's not as good as this one, or a sweater that laughs in the face of fashion. Put aside gifts you don't like or can't use, and regift them later. Then you can be an eco-friendly gift giver too!

SAY THIS IS THE LAST STRAW

For most people, they're unnecessary, and they're wreaking havoc on ocean wildlife. It's time to ditch plastic straws!

People in the United States use around 500 million drinking straws every day. Each one is used for just a few minutes before it's thrown away. Like all plastic litter, straws often end up in the ocean, where they take more than 200 **YEARS** to break down. In fact, straws are

PLANET-O-METER

one of the top 10 items found in beach cleanups—and that's the best-case scenario. Plastic straws have been found lodged in the nostrils of sea turtles and tangled in the stomachs of penguins. You get the picture—straws suck.

Up to 90 percent of the world's seabirds have plastic in their guts.

Some cities and countries have already banned plastic straws, and more plan to follow suit. They may be replaced by more eco-friendly alternatives, including straws made from paper, straws made from metal, and even straws made from straw! This is not a new idea—in fact, the very first drinking straws were the hollow stalks of plants! They were replaced by paper that was waxed to make it waterproof, and eventually by plastic. Several companies are reintroducing biodegradable, compostable straws, but these still have to be manufactured and transported to stores and homes, sucking up resources along the way. The best action is to say no to straws altogether.

THIS ROCK IS NOT GARBAGE

Forget about fidget spinners, loom bands, slime, and Pokémon. The biggest craze sweeping the planet is painted pebbles!

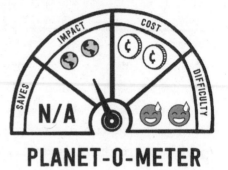

PLANET-O-METER

Look carefully when you're out and about, and you might spot a rock that doesn't look like all the others. Rocks painted with bright pictures and patterns have been popping up all over the country in all sorts of places—in parks, behind bushes, under trees, and on beaches.

Many have a message on the bottom, encouraging the finder to share a picture of the rock on social media before hiding it again or to paint a rock of their own.

Why not start your own rock-painting project with an eco-message? Seek out some rocks or pebbles and decorate them with waterproof, environmentally friendly paints. (Avoid spray paints, which are not kind to the planet.) On the bottom of each rock, include an eco-tip and the hashtag **#ThisRockIsNotGarbage**. Hide the rocks in your neighborhood and then spread the word. When people find a rock, they will be able to look up the hashtag and see even more eco-tips!

ECO-WORRIERS WARRIORS

START A FIGHT AT SCHOOL

Be an eco-warrior, not an eco-worrier.

PLANET-O-METER

Team up with some like-minded classmates and set up a school eco squad. It's a great way to multiply your planet-saving efforts **AND** spend more time with your friends. Think of yourselves as the eco-Avengers! Plan a term's worth of activities, and ask a teacher to lend a hand. If you can't start a club, why not ask a member of your student council to suggest similar actions? Or plan a school-wide assembly to share your ideas and inspire your whole school to play their part in saving the planet.

10 IDEAS TO KICK-START YOUR ECO SQUAD

1 Form a litter-picking team to fight trash in your local area.

2 Plant a wildflower meadow at school.

3 Transform junk into gifts to sell at a school fundraiser.

4 Make posters to encourage people to bicycle or walk to school.

5 Start a #ThisRockIsNotGarbage project (see pages 56–57).

6 Conduct a green audit to find out how much your school is already doing to save the planet.

7 Build a giant bug hotel using old wooden pallets and natural materials.

8 Hang homemade bird feeders outside at school (see pages 89–91).

9 Post paper-saving and recycling ideas (see pages 142–145) next to every photocopier, trash can, and supply closet.

10 Plant a vegetable garden on school grounds.

MAKE A PILE OF GARBAGE

Starting a compost pile is an easy way to harness the planet's own recycling power!

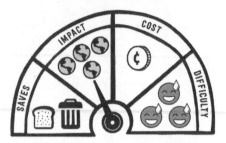

PLANET-O-METER

A compost pile is basically a massive heap of trash. Or, if you want to be fancy, "organic waste." You can chuck almost anything that used to be alive on it, from fruit peels, stale bread, and eggshells to grass clippings, paper, and cardboard. You can even compost your hair clippings! Putting it all in one big pile speeds up the natural chemical reactions that recycle dead stuff into the ingredients for new life. Compost piles also provide a toasty-warm home for animals that are very much alive, including earthworms, slugs, snails, millipedes, and even grass snakes. It's basically a free ticket to your very own creepy-crawly safari park!

Once the compost is ready, it helps plants grow more quickly and easily. Unlike store-bought fertilizers or mulch, homemade compost is free! It also comes without plastic packaging or the energy cost of transporting it to your home. It turns out that compost isn't garbage at all!

COUNTDOWN
TO CREATING YOUR
OWN COMPOST

5. To avoid attracting rats, build your compost pile on top of a sheet of chicken wire or mesh. You can add walls and a lid, but make sure it gets plenty of air.

4. Keep a little container in the kitchen especially for food scraps, and empty it straight onto your compost heap. This means less food waste goes in the trash.

3. Keep meat, oil, and dairy products out of the compost pile to avoid attracting nasty pests.

2. You can put pet poop on the compost pile, but only if your pet is vegetarian.

1. When the waste has become crumbly compost, it can be scattered all over the garden or mixed into the soil you use for houseplants.

DON'T RUSH TO FLUSH!

How often do you flush the toilet? In a survey, 63 percent of people said they flush after every pee. Science says this is too often.

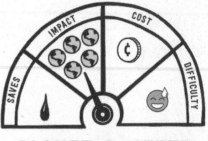

PLANET-O-METER

More than one-quarter of the water we use at home goes straight down the toilet! Researchers at Indiana University have shown that flushing less often could reduce our water usage and bills much more than turning off the water while brushing our teeth, or even taking shorter showers (see page 23), can.

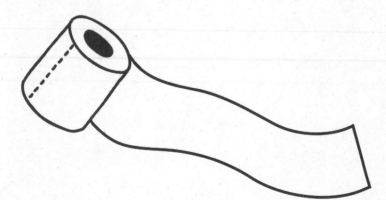

If it's yellow, let it mellow.

OFFICIALLY BACKED BY SCIENCE!

If your family isn't convinced, there are other things you can do. If you have an older, larger toilet tank, ask if you can pop in a brick or an air-filled bag that stops the tank from filling with more water than needed. Some water companies provide these "hippo" devices for free, and they can save more than a day's worth of drinking water **PER FLUSH**.

If it's brown, flush it down!

Even easier is taking your first pee of the day in the shower! This was the focus of recent campaigns in Brazil and the United Kingdom. Urine is totally germ-free, so as long as the water is flowing, it's perfectly clean. And it's all headed for the same place anyway: the sewers. Taking just one pee in the shower each day could save 600 gallons of water in a year—enough to fill a hot tub! (Though we definitely don't recommend doing that—the hot tub is another eco-enemy!)

Don't worry about adding too much extra
time to your shower, either. Humans only
take an average of 21 seconds to pee!

IT'S A WRAP

If you've planned the perfect eco-friendly gift, don't ruin all your good work by covering it in sheets of wrapping paper that will be ripped off in seconds and never used again.

PLANET-O-METER

In the United Kingdom, people throw away almost 250,000 miles of wrapping paper at Christmas alone—enough to wrap the planet (around the equator) **10** times. Stuffing it into the recycling bin doesn't undo the damage. Most wrapping paper contains plastic film, foil, and glitter, not to mention sticky tape, so it can't be recycled. Try one of these ideas instead:

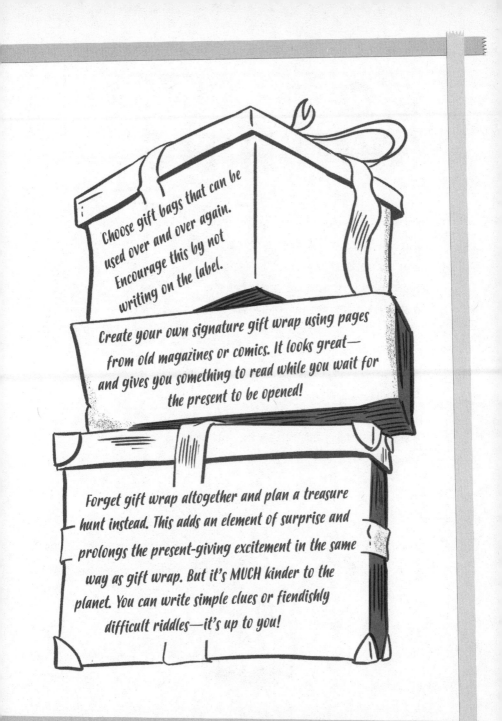

Choose gift bags that can be used over and over again. Encourage this by not writing on the label.

Create your own signature gift wrap using pages from old magazines or comics. It looks great—and gives you something to read while you wait for the present to be opened!

Forget gift wrap altogether and plan a treasure hunt instead. This adds an element of surprise and prolongs the present-giving excitement in the same way as gift wrap. But it's MUCH kinder to the planet. You can write simple clues or fiendishly difficult riddles—it's up to you!

GO SWISHING

A swish—or clothes-swapping party—is a fun and free way to update your wardrobe without putting a strain on the planet.

PLANET-O-METER

Stores in shopping malls are full of cheap, disposable clothes—and so are landfill sites. WRAP (the Waste and Resources Action Programme in the UK) has done some detective work and discovered that fashion is environmental enemy number four, after housing, transportation, and food (which are harder to give up!).

ENVIRONMENTAL
ENEMY
#4

IN THE UNITED STATES, THE AVERAGE SHOPPER
BUYS 68 GARMENTS EVERY YEAR. AND EVERY
YEAR, WE THROW AWAY A TOTAL OF
12.8 MILLION TONS OF CLOTHING AND FOOTWEAR.
JUST 1.7 MILLION TONS OF THIS IS RECYCLED—
8.9 MILLION TONS GOES INTO LANDFILLS.
THAT'S HARD TO IMAGINE, BUT PICTURE THIS:

☆ 181,000 tractor trailer loads of cotton, nylon, and sequins
being dumped into holes in the ground

Producing and then washing all these clothes . . .

☆ releases as much carbon dioxide into the atmosphere
as every family in the United States driving a car for
6,000 miles each year.

☆ uses enough water to fill 1,000 bathtubs per family per year.

For every single ton of clothing made, another 1.7 tons of waste is left behind.

To make sure our passion for fashion doesn't keep stripping the planet of resources, we need to love and value our clothes more. This means keeping them out of landfills by making small repairs, wearing the same item more often, and giving clothes a longer life—even if that's in someone else's wardrobe. One of the easiest ways to do this is to swish. . . .

SWISH . . .

In the United States, people recycle only
15 percent of their used clothing.

SWISH . . .

COUNTDOWN TO A SWISH

5. Choose a date and time. Send an e-invite to friends who like similar clothes. Ask them to gather clothes and accessories that they no longer wear or use but that are in good, clean condition.

4. As people arrive, swap their donations for tokens. You can use cardboard counters.

3. Display all the donations for everyone to browse. Why not put out some drinks and snacks, too?

2. When you're ready, draw straws (not plastic ones!) to decide who goes first. Take turns swapping your tokens for new-to-you items.

1. If anything is left over, donate it to a local charity.

Swishing isn't just for clothes. Include accessories, books, sports gear, and toys—anything that you've grown bored of but that someone else might like to use.

LET YOUR BACKYARD GET MESSY

When it comes to gardening, less is more. . . .

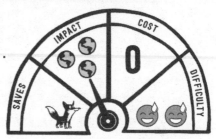

PLANET-O-METER

There's nothing wildlife hates more than a neatly mowed lawn. Lock up the lawn mower, ditch the weeding, and let the (leaf) litter pile up.

COUNTDOWN TO A REALLY WILD YARD

Ask for permission and help from an adult to follow these steps.

5. Stop mowing an area of grass over the summer, and let it grow long. Even 10 square feet will let wildflowers grow and give small animals a place to hide.

4. Instead of cultivated flowers (which often produce little nectar and pollen), scatter native wildflower seeds to create a meadow border. You'll attract insects, which in turn will attract birds and bats.

3. Make small holes under fences so animals can pass easily from yard to yard.

2. Don't pick up fallen leaves and dead wood. Piles of leaves, twigs, or logs are cozy homes for hibernating animals.

1. Dig a small pond and turn an ordinary backyard into a wildlife haven!

SAVE THE PLANET WHILE YOU SLEEP

More electricity than ever is being generated from renewable sources, including solar, wind, biomass, and hydropower. However, they account for less than 4 percent of the energy used in the United States. So there's still a long way to go.

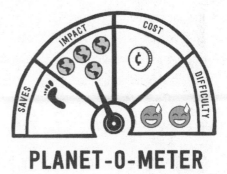

PLANET-O-METER

Also, most of this "green" electricity can only be generated during the day or when it's windy. At times of high demand—like on a summer afternoon, when the air-conditioning is cranked up—only fossil fuel–burning, greenhouse gas–belching power stations can deal with the surge in demand.

You can help by refusing to do any chores that involve electricity . . . but only at peak times! Save your chores for times of low demand instead. Ditto for devices that plug in. Make sure they're not left on standby during times of peak demand.

In general, the late afternoon and early evening are times of peak power demand, when people come home from school and work and switch on lights, TVs, and ovens. We generally use less electricity at night, when most people are asleep. This is a good time to run washing machines and dishwashers and to charge devices such as tablets and phones. In the future, smart devices that can collect and share data with each other (known as the Internet of Things, or IoT) will probably make these decisions for us. In the meantime, you can find out the best and worst times of day to use electricity at

EIA.GOV/TODAYINENERGY /DETAIL.PHP?ID=42915

or ask your electricity supplier.

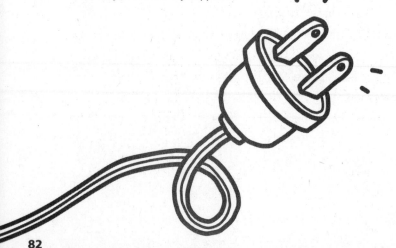

It might seem like a small change, but if enough families follow this advice, it could mean fewer new power stations will need to be built!

About one-fourth of electricity generated around the world comes from renewable sources.

DON'T HAND IN YOUR HOMEWORK . . .

. . . email it instead! When it comes to schoolwork, tell your teacher that more screen time actually *could* save the planet.

More than 400 million tons of paper are produced each year—the equivalent of 230 rolls of toilet paper for everyone on the planet. Of course, it's not all toilet paper. About one-quarter of the total is printing and writing paper. Making this paper involves cutting down 4 billion trees each year. Trees may be renewable, but the energy, water, and chemicals involved in making paper give it a hefty carbon footprint.

PLANET-O-METER

One easy way to reduce the amount of paper we use is to stop wasting it. The average UK family throws away six trees' worth of paper every year, while in the United States, a billion trees' worth of paper is thrown away each year. Globally, about two-thirds of paper is recycled, which is great, but paper is still one of the most common waste items in landfills.

Paper is also the main type of waste created by schools. We need paper in schools—to share ideas, practice new skills, and be creative. But saving the planet means finding different ways to work. Try some of these ideas:

☆ Suggest that your teacher contact families and assign homework via email.

☆ Ask if you can do your homework digitally and email it to your teacher.

☆ Use a little whiteboard for making notes and drafts.

☆ Rather than photocopying something, take a photograph and store it digitally.

☆ Always use both sides of a piece of paper, and finish a notebook before starting a new one.

Use a whiteboard!

☆ Set up a scrap paper drawer in each classroom, and recycle any paper that can't be used as scrap.

☆ Think before you print: Can you read it on-screen?

☆ Print only the page or section you need.

☆ Set your printer default to double-sided printing.

☆ Reuse old drawings and drafts as wrapping paper. (After all, it's the thought that counts.)

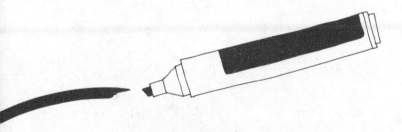

The pulp and paper industry is the fifth-largest consumer of energy in the world. It makes up 4 percent of the world's total energy consumption!

BE A BIRD BRAIN

Where have all the insects gone? You're not the only one wondering. Birds rely on creepy-crawlies for every meal.

PLANET-O-METER

Once upon a time, every long car ride would end with a windshield splattered with insects that were flying in the wrong place at the wrong time. Today's cars tend to stay much cleaner, which is good news if you're responsible for washing the car, but terrible news for the planet.

A huge study published in 2020 showed that in the last 30 years, the world has lost more than a quarter of the population of insects that live on land. The declines were strongest in Europe and in the Midwestern United States, which has lost 4 percent of its insects every year since 1990. Habitat loss, changes in land use, and the chemicals that farms pour onto fields are partly to blame. This isn't just bad news for the insects, either. Many other animals—especially birds—eat insects.

You can give birds a helping hand by putting up a bird feeder in your yard. Even better news? It's easy to make one from junk—another way to help the planet! Here are two plans to make your own. Ask an adult to help you.

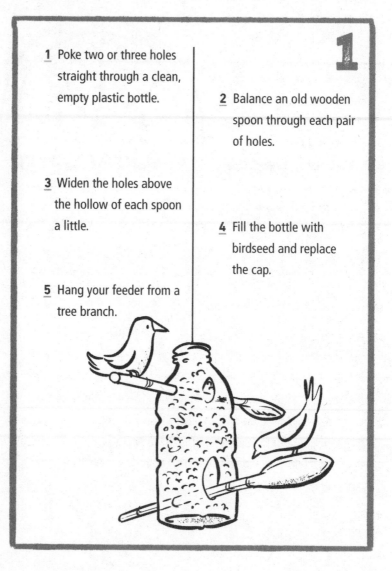

1 Poke two or three holes straight through a clean, empty plastic bottle.

2 Balance an old wooden spoon through each pair of holes.

3 Widen the holes above the hollow of each spoon a little.

4 Fill the bottle with birdseed and replace the cap.

5 Hang your feeder from a tree branch.

1 Cut a hole in the side of a clean, empty plastic milk jug.

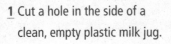

2 Poke a small hole just underneath the larger hole, to hold a little stick or a pencil.

3 Fill the base with birdseed and replace the cap. Hang the jug from the branch of a tree.

USE YOUR BUTT

It's not a rainy day—it's a free-water day! Here's how to make the most of it.

PLANET-O-METER

It might not feel like it when your visit to the BMX track is rained out for the fourth day in a row, but fresh water is a precious and scarce resource. More than 97 percent of Earth's water is salty, and while

it looks lovely from space, it doesn't help quench the thirst of the 6.5 million species of plants and animals that live on land.

We can drink only the remaining 2.5 percent—or 2.5 million cubic miles—of fresh water. This sounds like a lot, but if you think of it as 10 glasses full of water:

Almost seven are frozen as snow and ice ....

More than three are hidden underground ....

Leaving just a few drops of water, which are found in lakes, swamps, rivers, reservoirs, and streams ....

. . . and we all have to share it.

About half of the world's population already lives in areas where there isn't enough water. And even in countries where it rains a lot, the water supply is often stretched in the summer. This makes water one of the world's most precious resources.

Every drop you can save helps. Even better, invest in a rain barrel, also known as a water butt, and harvest this liquid gold for free!

COUNTDOWN to WATER CONSERVATION

5. A rain barrel is the easiest way to collect lots of rainwater. Check that you're allowed to install one in your area. The barrel usually comes with a kit to collect all the water running down a drainpipe.

4. Make sure your barrel has a lid to keep animals and small children from falling in. Add a teaspoon of vegetable oil to sit on the surface to stop mosquitoes or flies from breeding.

3. Plants don't need water that has been treated to make it safe for humans to drink. Rainwater can actually be better for them. Fill a water pistol and give your houseplants a good soaking.

2. Use rainwater to wash the car—or even to flush the toilet!

1. Don't drink the water you collect or use it for water fights.

About 26,417 gallons of rainwater falls onto
the average roof EACH YEAR!
And most goes straight into the sewers.

BE A TREE HUGGER

For immediate eco-impact, you can't do better than planting a tree. And if you can't plant one, adopt one!

PLANET-O-METER

Trees are the biggest plants on the planet, and they're vital for life as we know it. As they photosynthesize (make food for themselves, aided by the energy in sunlight), they soak up the greenhouse gas carbon dioxide, trapping it in their trunks, branches, roots, and leaves. The only waste product is oxygen, the gas that keeps every other creature alive. How amazing is that?!

Tree canopies improve the air in other ways, too, catching dust and dangerous pollutants, which are then washed away by rain. Trees protect habitats from soil erosion, floods, and drought—and provide habitats for millions of other living things.

For hundreds of thousands of years, trees have provided the materials for human shelter, tools, and fire. For medicines, musical instruments, and furniture. For paper, rubber, and cork. For a good place to hide when being chased by hyenas. Is that all trees can do? No—science has shown that just looking at trees can help us feel less stressed! Unless, of course, you **ARE** being chased by a hyena.

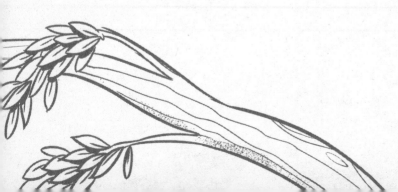

Pick a tree to adopt, either in your backyard or somewhere near enough to visit weekly. Then just . . . look. Watch how it changes through the year. Notice which creatures call it home. (A single oak tree can boast up to 500 different species!) You haven't adopted just one plant but an entire **ECOSYSTEM**!

10 WAYS TO MAKE YOUR TREE FEEL LOVED

1 Hug it.

2 Climb it (if it's safe and appropriate—and always ask an adult to supervise).

3 Measure it. Standing a few hundred yards away, hold out your hand so it looks like you're pinching your tree with your thumb at the base of the trunk and your forefinger at the very top of the crown. Carefully turn your hand ninety degrees, keeping your fingers the same space apart, until your forefinger appears to touch the ground (but your thumb is still at the base of the trunk). Note the spot marked by your forefinger, then measure the actual distance between that spot and the trunk to find the height of your tree.

4 Identify it. Use clues like the shape and size of leaves, and compare them with pictures in a book.

5 Preserve it. Take leaf rubbings, or collect and press leaves between sheets of newspaper and cardboard.

6 Frame it. Take a picture of the tree each week from the same spot. You could make a video, too—turn the pics into a time-lapse clip showing how the tree changes over the year.

7 Art it. Create natural art using materials from your tree, such as fallen leaves, needles, twigs, keys, or pine cones.

8 Science it. Hunt for microhabitats and find out what's hiding there. Try cracks in the bark, holes between roots, the undersides of leaves, and inside any bulges (known as galls).

9 Clone it. Take cuttings from your tree (if you have permission from the owner) and give them as gifts.

10 Plant it. For extra eco-points, plant a tree of your own.

CHALK IT UP

Twenty-first-century people have a bad habit of buying more "stuff" as soon as we feel bored. But instead of always looking for the new, try revisiting the past. . . .

What did we do for fun in a world before plastic dart guns, plastic wading pools, and plastic sports equipment? Okay, so hoop rolling or playing soccer with a pig's bladder probably isn't going to catch on anytime soon, but some of the old ideas are worth revisiting—especially as they tend to be more environmentally friendly.

PLANET-O-METER

Chalk, for example. Chalk is a natural material, made from gypsum or limestone. This means it can be used outside without harming wildlife. It creates little waste, since it all gets used up, and it often has simple, recyclable packaging. Invest in a pack of colored chalk and you can create your own fun without reaching for a new toy. . . .

COUNTDOWN TO CALCIUM CARBONATE FUN

5. Chalk a target or goal on a wall, instead of buying plastic ones.

4. Chalk enormous versions of board games on a driveway or patio.

3. Use chalk to create an eco-friendly treasure trail along a sidewalk.

2. Paint a section of wall or a piece of furniture with eco-friendly blackboard paint. Chalk reminders and lists instead of using paper.

1. Mix chalk and water and paint your own (temporary) mural.

DON'T

DOODLE IN CHALK ON PUBLIC PAVEMENTS OR WALLS—THIS IS ILLEGAL IN SOME COUNTRIES.

TAKE A BAG FOR A WALK

When is a plastic bag not an eco-villain? When it swaps sides and helps rid the world of litter!

PLANET-O-METER

Litter is bad news for wildlife. It also looks disgusting and quickly turns beautiful scenes into no-go zones . . . which encourages people to drop even more litter!

The main things dropped by litterbugs in the United States are cigarette butts, paper, leftover food, wrappers, napkins, soda cans, cups, and plastic bottles. Obviously, one of the easiest ways you can help is by not being a litterbug yourself. But you can have an even bigger impact by helping clean up after the 62 percent of the population (that's almost two in every three people!) who admit to dropping litter.

Cleaning up nature is a lot more fun than cleaning your bedroom! You can wear cool clothes, use a mechanical grabber, or even combine your cleanup with a treasure hunt. So the next time a plastic bag makes its way into your house, take it on a walk. It could be a stroll in the park, a woodland wander, or just a five-minute dash around a patch of land near your home. Aim to fill the bag with litter. Each piece you pick up could prevent a bird from choking on a balloon, a shrew from suffocating in a plastic bag, or a hedgehog from getting its head stuck in a container. This kind of cleaning up can save lives!

More than 51 billion pieces of litter are dropped along US roads each year. This is even more shocking when you realize that littering is illegal in every state and can be punished with a fine— or worse.

COUNTDOWN TO A LITTER BLITZ

5. Take two bags if possible, so you can separate recyclable and nonrecyclable litter.

4. Bend wire coat hangers into a diamond shape and use them to hold your bags open.

3. Look for opportunities to join a group litter cleanup, or to join in a virtual event such as #2MinuteBeachClean. It's fun to share your haul!

2. Recycle as much of the litter as you can. (This is MUCH easier if you separate the litter as you go.)

1. Stay safe—read the tips on the next page.

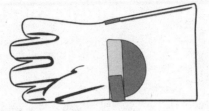

STAYING SAFE

Never go litter picking on your own—always take at least one adult with you. (They're also handy for carrying the garbage!) Wear bright, protective clothing and tough gloves (such as gardening gloves). Never pick up broken glass. Alert the police about illegal dumping or any needles you come across and stop collecting in that area. Choose a safe location to litter pick, and avoid roads—you won't be able to look out for traffic while you're gathering trash. Afterward, wash your hands well with soap and water—even if you wore gloves.

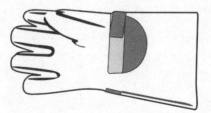

SAY "NO THANK YOU" CARDS

It's great to get gifts, especially if they're eco-kind (see pages 50–51). But nothing spoils the vibe like feeling guilty for forgetting to write thank-you cards.

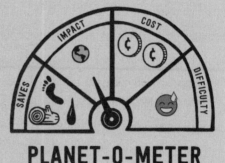

PLANET-O-METER

Well, say goodbye to guilt! Every time you don't send a greeting card—from thank-you notes to birthday cards—you're doing the planet a huge favor.

It's not just the paper used to make the cards that's the problem. Lots of energy and chemicals go into making those brightly colored pictures, giving them a glossy coating, and gluing on glitter to make them stand out in the store. And to make matters even worse, many cards are sold in plastic sleeves.

If you must buy cards, look for those made from sustainable forests or recycled paper. Or, even better, try these alternative ways to show someone you care.

TOP 10 CARD-BUSTING ALTERNATIVES

1 Make a phone call.

2 Send an e-card or a video greeting—ask an adult to make sure it's from a safe source!

3 Make your own card using stuff you find around the house.

4 Send a letter or a drawing.

5 Send a postcard. (Envelope glue has an eco-impact too.)

6 Write a special message in chalk (see pages 104–105).

7 Bake and decorate a cake or some cupcakes—cuter (and tastier) than a card.

8 Print a favorite photo and write a message on the back.

9 Take a leaf from the ancient Romans' book and send, er, leaves! They used to exchange branches from olive and laurel trees, but you could give someone a cutting to plant.

10 Save any cards you receive and reuse the pictures as thank-you notes.

Americans send more greeting cards than
people in other countries do. In the past decade,
people in the United States bought 7 billion cards
each year—spending a total of $7.5 billion!

EAT MORE FRIES!
(OVEN-BAKED FRIES, THAT IS)

They might seem fairly harmless, sitting quietly in the dark, but potatoes are doing their part to destroy the planet.

PLANET-O-METER

Potatoes have the 10th-biggest carbon footprint of all foods. Every 2 pounds of potatoes your family eats releases the equivalent of 6.4 pounds of carbon dioxide into the atmosphere—more than any other protein-rich plant food.

More than 80 percent of these emissions are due to the energy and time it takes to cook potatoes. Baking a large potato for an hour is much worse for the environment than cooking oven fries for 20 minutes.

So eat more fries—science says so!

COTTON ON TO CLOTHING WASTE

PLANET-O-METER

From sports uniforms to souvenirs to your comfy weekend wardrobe, there are bound to be a few cotton T-shirts hanging out in your closet. Don't ignore them— they're slowly destroying the planet.

Cotton comes from plants, so it must be better for the environment than synthetic fabrics, right? Not necessarily. Cotton is one of the most high-maintenance crops in the world—imagine the Kardashians AND the British royals in plant form, and you'll get the picture. It takes more than 700 gallons of water to make a single cotton T-shirt. That's enough drinking water to keep a person alive for nearly 2.5 **YEARS**. Cotton production also uses more pesticides than any other single crop. That's a vat of chemicals dumped on the land just so that someone can wear a slogan tee.

Cotton doesn't stop being thirsty once it's in your wardrobe, either. Many people only wear denim jeans an average of two or three times before washing them. That adds up to 198 gallons of water to wash just one pair of jeans over its lifetime.

We also need to stop thinking of cotton as disposable. Whether it's last-year's grass-stained jersey or a too-small tie-dyed tee, there's bound to be at least one piece of cotton clothing you no longer wear but can't donate or swish (see pages 72–77). Find another way to stop that cotton from going to waste. Try these ideas on for size.

GLUG
GLUG
GLUG

COUNTDOWN TO A LONGER LIFE FOR COTTON

5. Reduce the impact of cotton at home by wearing T-shirts and jeans just one more time before tossing them onto the laundry pile (assuming you haven't just finished a mud run in them!). This will help them last longer, too.

4. Avoid tumble drying and ironing cotton clothes, to reduce their carbon footprint.

3. Cotton jersey doesn't fray. If you've outgrown a T-shirt or just gotten sick of it, try cutting a new neckline or sleeves. *Et voilà!* A brand-new top!

2. Cut old cotton into long strips and braid them together—you've got an instant hairband, belt, or pet toy.

1. Look up instructions for making pom-poms and use cotton strips instead of wool. You only need scissors, scrap cardboard, and the ability to tie a knot. String your pom-poms together to make garlands, decorate an old cushion with them, or even use them to replace sponges.

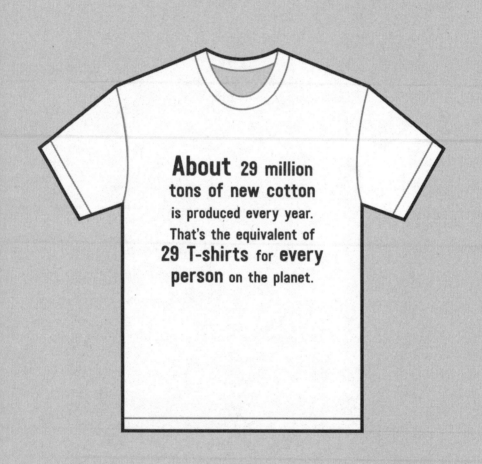

About 29 million tons of new cotton is produced every year. That's the equivalent of 29 T-shirts for every person on the planet.

TAKE YOUR JUNK FOR A HOT CHOCOLATE...

. . . at a repair café! And if you can't find one, start your own.

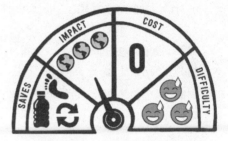

PLANET-O-METER

Think twice before you ditch anything with a battery or a plug. The United Nations has warned that electronic waste, or e-waste, is a MAJOR threat to the environment and to human health. But we generate about 50 million tons of it every year.

This mountain of mobile phones, laptops, TVs, electronic toys, flat irons, fairy lights, e-readers, and lamps is packed full of valuable materials like gold, silver, copper, and platinum. It's more like jewels than junk! No single item would look like a glittering treasure chest if you opened it up, but together the e-waste thrown away in a single year contains materials worth almost $50 billion that could be recovered and reused. Yet just 20 percent of this potential gold (silver, copper, and platinum) mine is being recycled.

We also throw away piles of things that could be fixed, which is where repair cafés come in. There are more than 1,500 repair cafés around the world, run by volunteers who can help you bring broken stuff back to life—for free! Their aim is to reduce the amount of waste going to landfills and shrink the carbon footprint of buying new stuff.

Repair cafés aren't just for electronic items—anything from bicycles and stuffed animals to jeans and jewelry can be mended while you relax with a hot drink. You'll learn new skills, so you can pass the knowledge on.

Visit
REPAIRCAFE.ORG
to see if there is one in your area.
If not, ask your school or youth group
if you can start your own. Your local
government may also be willing to help.

DRAFT BUSTERS

MIND THE GAP

PLANET-O-METER

There's something strange in your neighborhood. It's silent and invisible but gives you goose bumps and sends a shiver down your spine. Who you gonna call? Draft busters!

Drafts may be small, but they can add up to a house-sized problem. Even the tiniest gaps can let warm air leak out of our homes, and cold air flows in to take its place. This lowers the room temperature, meaning the furnace has to burn more fuel. Drafts also make us feel colder than we really are, tempting us to turn up the heat.

It can be fun to hunt for drafts. Wait for a cold day (a breeze makes it even easier), then hold a feather near one of these Draft Danger Zones:

☆ external doors

☆ keyholes

☆ mail slot

☆ attic door

☆ cellar door

☆ unused chimneys

☆ windows

☆ cat and dog doors

☆ gaps between floorboards

☆ gaps under the baseboards

☆ anywhere pipes leave the house

If you feel the flow of cold air or see your feather flutter, take action. You can buy draft stoppers, but it's just as easy to fill small gaps with rolled-up newspaper. For larger gaps, try stuffing one leg of an old pair of tights with fabric or paper scraps to make a draft stopper. A rolled-up rug or blanket will also work well. You'll be reusing waste materials, too! Plug the gaps and you should be able to turn the heat down and save on energy bills. Great news for your novelty-sweater fund (see pages 140–141).

When filling gaps, be sure not to cover up air vents. They do an important job letting fresh air circulate.

WHOOSH!

THINK LIKE A SEA TURTLE

What's the difference between a plastic bag and a jellyfish? It's no joke. Turtles really can't tell the difference, and their mistake is costing them their lives.

PLANET-O-METER

Plastic shopping bags are used for an average of 12 minutes. So it's totally sensible to make them from plastic designed to last 500 years. Right?*

*Did you spot the error in this logic? Congratulations, that puts you one step ahead of most of the world's population. Up to 1 trillion single-use plastic bags are used around the world each year—that's nearly **2 MILLION** every minute!

Each bag is the start of a sad story. About 8 million tons of plastic ends up in the world's oceans every year. Small animals get trapped inside plastic bags and suffocate. Large animals don't fare much better. A shark or seal has no hands to remove a shopping bag from around its neck. If a plastic bag blocks a fish's gills, the fish can no longer breathe oxygen from the water, and it suffocates.

Marine animals are eating more and more plastic. One study of seabirds found that 9 in 10 had plastic in their stomachs, and not just a little bit—more than 36 pieces per bird! Turtles and beaked whales are known to eat plastic bags, mistaking them for jellyfish or squid. Even nonpredatory, filter-feeding whales are swallowing plastic bags that drift into their enormous mouths. Globally, up to a million seabirds and 100,000 marine mammals and sea turtles die each year from eating plastic.

The bad news? We are all responsible for the problem. The good news? We can all help solve it. Small changes add up to a BIG difference. Take a cloth bag or a backpack with you every time you head for the stores. Carry snacks in reusable boxes instead of sandwich bags. Next time a store clerk asks "Would you like a bag?" channel your inner sea turtle and say no.

Governments around the world have introduced bans or fees to limit plastic-bag use, and they really work. Even a small charge can make a big difference. Before a fee was introduced in Britain, each person used, on average, 140 bags per year. In just one year, this fell to about 25 bags per year. And in Denmark, where plastic bags have been taxed for more than 25 years, people use an average of just four bags per year.

GET ON YOUR BIKE (OR SKATES, OR SCOOTER . . .)

Every time you ride in a car, the exhaust fumes leave an invisible trail of greenhouse gases and other unpleasant things in your wake.

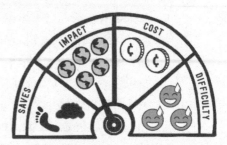

PLANET-0-METER

These include toxic gases such as carbon monoxide, as well as tiny particles and droplets of hundreds of chemicals. Some of these particles are so small, you could line up 10 across a single human hair (if you had *really* tiny tweezers). There's no way to avoid inhaling these particles, and over time they get lodged in our lungs and can seriously damage our health. Children are most at risk because their lungs are still growing.

This type of air pollution is such a serious issue that idling (leaving the engine running while a vehicle is not moving) is against the law in some places. Experiments have shown that staying inside the car doesn't help—in fact, air in the back seat of a car is up to 12 times as polluted as the air outside. This is because the car's ventilation system sucks in fumes, trapping them inside the car.

One solution is to drive less and walk or cycle more. Start by keeping a diary of every car trip you make for a week, including rides from other people. Which could you have made on two wheels (or two feet!) if you'd taken off a bit earlier? Swap in at least one walk or bike ride next week, and you'll be making a difference.

Although 52 percent of Americans have access to a bike, only about 14 million ride them regularly.

On your **BIKE!**

Stay safe. Get your bike checked to make sure it's roadworthy. Always wear bright or reflective clothes and a helmet when cycling. Cross roads carefully. Use lights after dusk.

DRESS TO IMPRESS

It's the easiest challenge in this book. You're probably doing it already!

PLANET-O-METER

Every time you hear a radiator or air-conditioning unit crank up, try to think of it as a boring-looking T-rex. Heating and cooling our homes gobbles up energy faster than you can say "Triceratops," and most of this energy still comes from fossil fuels—either directly or to make electricity.

If you're feeling too hot or too cold at home, visit your closet before you head for the thermostat. In cold weather, put on a sweater or a fleece—they're not just for outside! In warm weather, peel layers off before you decide to turn on the air-conditioning.

There are other easy things you can do, too. Don't dry wet clothes and towels on radiators. This lowers the room temperature and makes the boiler work harder. Put a rack near the radiator instead. Keep your curtains and furniture away from the radiator, too, and close your blinds or curtains as it starts to get dark, to keep heat from escaping.

If you're feeling super enthusiastic, why not check whether your heating system is wearing a sweater too? Wrapping insulation around hot-water tanks and exposed pipes will keep water hotter for longer, giving your furnace a break. (Use foam insulation rather than a knitted number.) It's an easy way to cut energy use and bills. Just think—you could use that extra money to buy a nice fluffy sweater!

APPOINT YOURSELF FAMILY CHIEF . . .

. . . of recycling.
(Everyone has to
start somewhere.)

PLANET-O-METER

Your mission, should you
choose to accept it, is to
keep everyone away from
the trash can. There are two ways you can do this. (**1**) By dropping in
some raw fish or ripe cheese on a hot day. Effective, but it won't
improve the kitchen environment. Or (**2**) do your homework,
research what can and can't be recycled in your area, and
post reminders absolutely **EVERYWHERE**.

COUNTDOWN TO
WASTE DOMINATION

5

Track how many trash bags your family puts out for each collection for a month, and see if you can get the number down.

MWAH HAH HAH HA

4

List all the types of garbage your family throws away: metal, compostable waste, glass, plastic, cooked food, batteries.... The easiest way to do this is to hang a tally chart by the trash can.

MWAH HAH HAH HA

3

Work through the list and identify where your family could be better at recycling. Then tell them if they really love you, they'll want to protect the planet that they are passing on to you by following your new rules.

MWAH HAH HAH HA

MWAH HAH HAH HA

MWAH HAH HAH HA

2

Make sure there is a small container in the kitchen for fruit and veggie scraps, coffee grounds, and tea bags. Use the contents to start a compost pile (see page 65).

MWAH HAH HAH HA

MWAH HAH HAH HA

1

Put a cardboard box next to the trash can to collect paper that's only been used on one side. Then transfer it to the printer.

DESIGN YOUR DREAM DEN

Upcycling is a great way to create a special space without costing the Earth (or all your pocket money).

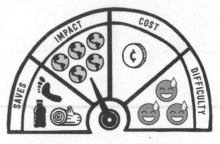

PLANET-O-METER

When we think about being energy efficient at home, saving heat and electricity springs to mind (see pages 81–83 and 140–141). But all your "stuff" has a carbon footprint, too.

From furniture to fairy lights, beanbags to board games, we all like to surround ourselves with nice things. And just as our clothes change, our tastes do too. No teenager wants (or fits) the same furniture they had as a toddler!

Each year, Americans alone throw out more than 57 million tons of furniture and other bulky waste. That's the weight of **2.8 BILLION** twin size mattresses. Even a princess couldn't feel a pea through that!

Most of this bulky waste is burned or buried in landfills. But furniture has great reuse potential. Right now, 80 percent of all furniture thrown away in the United States (including sofas, tables, and chairs) is landfilled. Almost 20 percent is burned. Only a tiny proportion is recycled. Surely we can do better!

If you want to give your room a makeover, consider upcyling! You can turn old furniture, thrift-store finds, or materials you have lying around the house into something amazing that looks brand-new and 100 percent you.

TOP 10 EASY
UPCYCLING PROJECTS

1 Paint all or part of a piece of furniture with eco-friendly blackboard paint to create a surface you can doodle on.

2 Use Japanese washi tape to add color and pattern to old furniture. It covers up dents and scratches, and it's made from sustainable natural fibers like rice and bamboo.

3 Use another Japanese export—origami—to make decorations. From colorful cranes to terrifying tarantulas, you can fold scrap paper into whatever floats your (paper) boat.

4 Look for secondhand stools or office chairs. It's surprisingly easy to add a brand-new cover using some of your favorite fabric and a staple gun.

5 Keep an eye out for "junk" that can be used in different ways. A flowerpot or wire trash can turned upside down might make a great bedside table.

6 Buy pictures from thrift stores, paint the frames in bright colors, and create your own gallery.

7 Use wallpaper to update an old dresser or other piece of furniture. It's not just for walls!

8 Instead of chucking an old lampshade, remove the fabric cover, paint the metal frame, and screw in a low-wattage light bulb.

9 Frame a single page from a monthly planner, and you can write on it again and again with an erasable pen.

10 Hang a piece of string and use wooden clothespins to display photos.

GO AROUND AND AROUND IN CIRCLES

With 7.6 billion people in the world, there are 15.2 billion feet! Use yours to kick waste off the agenda.

PLANET-O-METER

Most things that we buy move in a straight line. Think about it:

RAW MATERIAL → *FACTORY* → *STORE* → *YOUR HOME* → *DISPOSAL*

If something stops working, we replace it. In fact, many products are designed deliberately to fail after a certain amount of time or to be difficult to repair. Computer chips make it easy to program a limited life span. This helps the economy because it keeps people coming back to the stores to buy more items. But it's terrible for the planet.

So, what if the straight line were bent into a circle instead?

This is known as a circular economy. Businesses still make money, and people still get paid—but waste is eliminated. It means planning ahead so that reuse and recycling are built into product design. It means encouraging customers to return used or broken products so that the materials can be recovered and new versions don't have to be made from scratch. Look for signs of the circular economy popping up near you—including stores that pay you to bring back bottles and cans for recycling or that give you a discount if you return used clothes to reuse, resell, or recycle.

Some of the most exciting plans involve sneakers. More than 20 billion pairs of shoes are produced every year around the world, and less than 5 percent of these are recycled. Projects like Sport Infinity are trying to change this by creating athletic shoes that will never end up in the trash. Imagine soccer cleats made out of an inexhaustible 3D supermaterial. After your favorite player has finished with them, every ounce can be broken down and remolded to make new cleats—for you!

It might be some time before you find Lionel Messi's recycled cleats on your feet, but in the meantime, look for athletic shoes made of recycled materials—such as sneakers created from plastic waste collected on beaches in the Maldives! You can save the planet in style.

START SHOUTING NOW!

Don't wait until you're finished with school to start saving the planet—it might be too late. You can become a campaigner right now.

Get ready to meet some amazing kids who have taken action to tackle some of our biggest global problems.

PLANET-O-METER

FELIX FINKBEINER started campaigning to plant a million trees when he was just nine years old. Today, 12 years later, he runs an organization called Plant-for-the-Planet and has recruited more than 67,000 young "climate justice ambassadors" from all over the globe. Having smashed his original target, Felix is now aiming to get a trillion trees planted around the world!

Join Felix's team:

PLANT-FOR-THE-PLANET.ORG/EN/JOIN-IN/BECOME-AN-AMBASSADOR

ANN MAKOSINSKI began inventing when she was seven. After creating a flashlight that gets its energy from body heat and a mug that can charge a phone, she began winning awards and giving talks around the world—all while still in her teens!

XIUHTEZCATL MARTINEZ started advocating for the environment when he was six. He's organized more than 100 events around the world and was one of the youngest people ever to speak on a United Nations panel. He's also the youth director of Earth Guardians. Xiuhtezcatl asks, if you don't step up, who will?

EARTHGUARDIANS.ORG/XIUHTEZCATL

ELLA and **AMY MEEK** were shocked when they discovered how badly plastic affects life underwater. They set out to pick up 100,000 pieces of plastic litter and also founded Kids Against Plastic to shout about the problems with single-use plastic. They are looking for more children to join the Kids Against Plastic crew and fight for the planet.

KIDSAGAINSTPLASTIC.CO.UK

Are you feeling inspired? You could join an existing initiative or take the lead and start something new. A campaign to ban plastic water bottles from your school? Or to encourage more people to walk to school? A campaign to clean up litter in your local area? This book might give you ideas, but it's not the boss of you, so be your own eco-hero!

ONCE YOU'VE DECIDED WHAT TO FOCUS ON, TRY THESE THREE THINGS:

1 Raise funds by organizing a walk-a-thon or similar event, selling things you've made, or selling tickets to a show.

2 Get attention from people in office. They are in a position to change rules and laws. They are also elected to represent **YOUR** voice. Write to them or ask an adult to help you arrange a meeting, and tell them what you think.

3 Get your campaign in the news. Every time you organize an event or achieve something awesome, ask an adult to help you shout about it to the local press. Send a press release to newspapers, local radio and TV stations, and children's magazines.

LEAVE ONLY FOOTPRINTS

How many endangered animals can you name?

PLANET-O-METER

Chances are, you didn't manage to list all **31,000** species on the International Union for Conservation of Nature (IUCN) Red List. When we think about animals at risk of extinction, polar bears, rhinos, and tigers come to mind. But most are much smaller and much closer to home.

In the United States, they include grizzly bears, red wolves, Florida panthers, giant sea bass, and many types of tree snails, frogs, turtles, bats, and birds. If we don't take steps to protect our nearest neighbors, they will follow in the (doomed) footsteps of the brown bears, wolves, and lynx that used to roam around Britain.

While you can't hop on a plane to the Arctic and personally save a polar bear, you can make a big difference to the survival chances of your local wildlife. Just follow the tips on the next page whenever you're exploring nature. It's a walk in the park!

COUNTDOWN TO CARING FOR YOUR NEIGHBORS

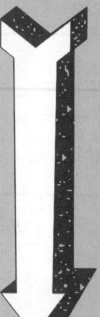

5. Carry all your garbage home, even biodegradable food waste. Anything you leave behind—from apple cores to cake crumbs—can disrupt an ecosystem.

4. Follow marked paths so you don't damage the plants that wildlife depend on.

3. Keep dogs on a leash.

2. No picking wildflowers. This is **SO** important that in many places it's against the law.

1. Don't pull bark off trees or carve your name or initials into the bark!

The IUCN's list of endangered animals, known as the Red List, is drawn from a survey of only 5 percent of Earth's living things, so the total number of threatened species is likely to be much higher.

BE A CITIZEN SCIENTIST

What do earthworms, penguins, and zombie flies have in common?

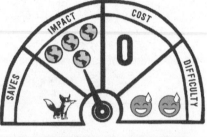

PLANET-0-METER

They've all been stared at by citizen scientists! These are people just like you who are interested in the world and its wildlife. They help researchers collect or analyze huge amounts of data that not even the brainiest professor could complete alone.

Citizen science is all about people power. Your observations will help scientists answer big questions about our planet and teach us how to protect it.

You don't need any training—just curiosity and access to an internet connection (earthworms need not apply). When you join a project, you'll be asked to carry out a specific task. You might be tagging penguins (cute!) or plastic litter (not so cute!) in photographs taken by robots. You might be looking out for honeybees infected by a parasitic fly that turns them into "zombees." Or you might be counting earthworms in your garden and logging the results on an app.

New projects start all the time, so you never know what you'll have the chance to do next. Search "citizen science" or check out the links below.

VISIT THESE WEBSITES TO LAUNCH YOUR SCIENCE CAREER / ZOMBIE FLY HUNT

SCISTARTER.COM

ZOONIVERSE.ORG

NHM.AC.UK/TAKE-PART
/CITIZEN-SCIENCE.HTML

DON'T BEE-LIEVE THE MYTHS

Zombees aside (see page 165), it's not a good time to be a bee.

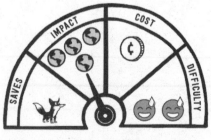

PLANET-O-METER

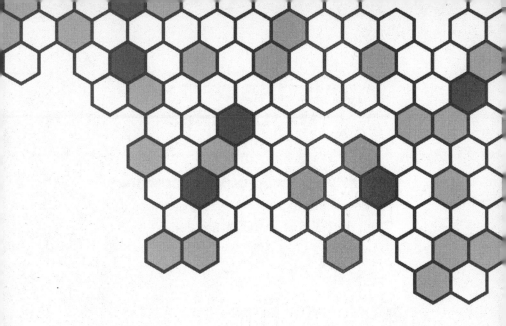

Bees aren't just a source of honey. They pollinate most of the world's flowering plants, including 84 percent of all the crops that humans eat. Plants don't start growing fruit until they've been pollinated, so without bees and other insects, there would be no chocolate, grapes, strawberries, or hundreds of other delicious foods. No brussels sprouts, either, but we'll keep that one quiet.

The work bees do is worth $160 billion to the world's economy, and they do it for free! We're not the only species that depends on bees. Their hard work props up entire ecosystems around the world. The scary thing is, the number of wild bees is falling fast. In 2017, the US Fish and Wildlife Service designated a bumblebee species as an endangered and protected species for the first time. A total of eight US bee species are facing extinction due to habitat loss, climate change, and invasive species.

BUSTING MYTHS ABOUT BEES

1 <u>THEY'RE ONLY AROUND IN SUMMER.</u>

There are 25,000 species of bees, and many are active all year round. This means you can help them at any time of the year.

2 <u>THEY LIVE IN BIG GROUPS.</u>

Most bees are solitary. They nest on their own, often in holes in the ground. Give them somewhere to nest by leaving patches of bare soil or building an insect hotel.

3 <u>THEY ONLY LIKE MESSY BACKYARDS.</u>

Bees would love it if you swapped your lawn for a mini-wildflower meadow (see pages 78–79), but they eat nectar and pollen from many other kinds of flowering plants, too. They love large areas of the same flower. Lavender, heather, abelia, mahonia, flowering trees, trees with catkins, and climbing plants like honeysuckle and ivy will bring bees to your garden all year round. Bees will also enjoy foraging from flowers in a vegetable garden—pollinating it for you in the process! If all else fails, just let some of your grass grow longer and encourage clover and dandelions instead of trying to get rid of them.

4 THEY ONLY NEED NECTAR AND POLLEN.

Bees need water too. A birdbath or small pond will help bring bees to your garden.

5 THEY LIKE TO STING.

Most female bees have stingers, but solitary bees are not at all aggressive. If you're careful, it's even possible to pet a bumblebee! But never disturb their nests, or they will become grumpy.

BECOME AN
ART-ACTIVIST

Could your artwork inspire other people to take action?

PLANET-O-METER

It's not just scientists who are key to saving the planet. Artists can be good at inspiring change, too. From toxic-sludge paintings to grasshopper burgers to 1,600 papier-mâché pandas snuggled up under the Eiffel Tower (yes, really), art has the power to make people pay attention to the problems our planet is facing.

You don't have to be a professional artist to get involved. One man in England simply collected every piece of plastic packaging he used in a year and turned them into a giant mural. He took it on a tour of the country, shocking people into using less.

YOU COULD TRY . . .

☆ Collecting all the milk jugs your family uses and turning them into a giant flock of plastic birds.

☆ Scooping up leftover acrylic paint and creating a mural (get permission first!) instead of pouring it down the drain.

☆ Gathering plastic bottle caps and lids, then using them to create a giant collage of circles.

Get your school involved and you'll be able to create something with an even bigger impact. Then ask your local newspaper to feature your creation to spread the word further.

DITCH THE RIDE TO SCHOOL

Not so fast! Before you recycle all your notebooks, please note that you *will* still have to go to school! You'll just need to find a better way to get there. . . .

PLANET-O-METER

Save money and get healthier without even trying. It sounds like a no-brainer—but the number of children walking to school is decreasing!

In the Netherlands, about 49 percent of children bicycle to and from school. In the United Kingdom, it's just 1 to 3 percent. So many journeys are made by car that the commute to school generates 2 million tons of carbon dioxide every year.

In the United States, many children are driven less than 2 miles to school. Are you one of them? If so, changing this habit can make a big difference—not only to the planet but also to your future. Walking, cycling, scooting, or skating to school leaves you more alert and ready to learn. Children who are more active even do better on tests than children who are driven to school. Not convinced yet? The average family could save $500 a year by going to school on foot!

Get other families involved, too, and you'll make walking safer for everyone. Ask your school to organize a walking bus (a group of children walking with one or more adults), a "walk once a week" challenge, or a park-and-stride program.

In the United States, 18 percent of kids who live within 2 miles of school get there by car.

READ THE LABEL
(AND SAVE A RAIN FOREST)

Eating meat and dairy is the fastest way to gobble up resources (see pages 10–14), but not all plants are as innocent as they look.

How often do you look at food labels when you grab a snack? It's the only way to catch these eco-baddies, which are replacing rain forests all around the globe.

PALM OIL is in about half of all packaged products. Huge areas of rain forest have been burned and cleared for planting oil palms instead. In Malaysia and Indonesia, where most of the world's palm oil comes from, rare rain forest species have been driven into smaller and smaller habitats. Native animals such as the orangutan are on the brink of extinction. But it's hard to avoid palm oil unless you cook everything from scratch. If you're choosing a snack at a store, look for products that are RSPO-certified. This means the palm oil they contain is from a sustainable source.

Nutri
Fact
Serving S
Calories
Fat Cal. 1
*Percent De
based one 2

PLANET-O-METER

COCOA is another crop responsible for wrecking rain forests. Most of the world's cocoa comes from West Africa. Even in some "protected" areas, 90 percent of the land has been cleared of tall rain forest trees for farming cocoa. In Côte d'Ivoire, there were once several hundred thousand forest elephants, but now just 200 to 400 survive in the country. It doesn't have to be this way. Cocoa plants can be grown in the shade of taller trees without chopping forests down. When you choose a chocolate bar, look for a little green frog. This shows that a crop is certified sustainable by the Rainforest Alliance.

Nutrition Facts		Amount/serving	%DV*	Amount/serving	%DV*
Serving Size 1 Bar		Total Fat 13g	20%	Total Carb. 26g	95%
Calories 210		Sat. Fat 8g	40%	Dietary Fibre 1g	4%
Fat Cal. 110		Trans Fat 0g		Sugars	24g
*Percent Daily Values (DV) are		Cholest. 10mg	3%	Protein	3g
based on a 2000 calorie diet.		Sodium 35mg	1%		

INGREDIENTS: MILK CHOCOLATE (SUGAR CANE, COCOA BUTTER, PALM OIL, LACTOSE, MILK FAT, SOY LECITHIN, EMULSIFIER, VANILLIN, ARTIFICIAL FLAVOUR).

REPLACING RAINFORESTS ALL AROUND THE GLOBE

SOYBEANS are a cheap source of protein, vegetable oil, and substances that make processed food last longer on the shelf. Produce from soybeans is "hidden" in about 70 percent of supermarket products, from bread to chocolate, and is also popular with fast-food chains. Most of the world's soy crops are used to feed farm animals—another reason to cut down on meat (see pages 10–14). Even people who hate soy sauce and avoid edamame beans could be eating up to 130 pounds of "hidden" soy every year. It's so popular with food manufacturers that rain forests in South America are rapidly being replaced with soybean plantations.

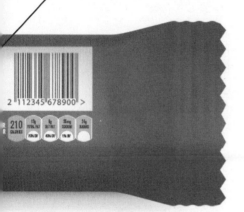

SUGARCANE is grown in more than 100 countries. The end product may be sweet, but the process of making it is not. Long after tropical rain forests are cleared to make way for sugarcane, nearby land and waterways are polluted by chemicals and sludge. It's the opposite of sweet. In fact, it's enough to leave a bitter taste in your mouth.

In South America's Amazon rain forest,
80 trees are cut down every four seconds;
64 of these are cleared to make way for farming.

CACHE IN

**You won't need a compass, a map, or a spade—
just a family member with a smartphone.**

Once you've found them and managed to drag their attention
from the screen, ask them to download the free geocaching app at
geocaching.com. Geocaches are little treasure troves that have
been hidden by people all over the world. Once you have the app,
you can use the world's global positioning system (GPS) to track
down geocaches.

PLANET-O-METER

Geocaching is a fun activity you'll want to do again and again. It's a great way to explore. As you look closely for caches or clues, you'll notice more wildlife, too.

Some caches are big enough to contain actual treasure. When you find one, you can take an item as long as you leave one behind. It's a fun way to reuse plastic gifts from party bags, instead of sending them to landfills.

Always take an adult with you and follow the tips on page 162 to make sure your geocaching walks don't harm wildlife. You can also take part in the Cache In, Trash Out! initiative, to leave your trail tidier than you found it. If you decide to get creative and hide your own geocache, follow the tips at geocaching.com to make sure it's environmentally friendly.

GAME OVER

If this book were a video game, this page would be the hardest level. Are you up for the challenge?

PLANET-O-METER

First the bad news: 91 percent of you play video games regularly, and the devices you play on are thirsty for energy. In the European Union, downloading and playing a typical game releases up to 17.5 pounds of carbon dioxide into the atmosphere. This is actually many times bigger than the carbon footprint of buying a game on a disc at a store.

Now the . . . actually, there's only bad news. Most of the tips in this book are about finding alternative ways to do the same thing. But the only way to make a difference in video-game land is to download less and play less.

What about playing games on a phone or tablet? Tablets use less energy to run than a console, laptop, or desktop computer and can be a good swap for things you'd normally do on paper (see pages 84–87). But downloading new content still has a big impact. Each time you do it, you're tapping into complex networks that involve energy-hungry collections of computer servers—and even satellites in space!

In the United States, game consoles use an estimated 16 billion kilowatt-hours of electricity per year—the same as a city of 1.4 million people.

COUNTDOWN TO GAMING THAT WON'T COST THE EARTH

5. Unplug devices when you have finished playing or downloading.

4. Don't leave your device on for downloads while you are out of the house or asleep.

3. Download games during off-peak times (see pages 81–83).

2. If possible, download games when your device is in standby mode.

1. Think carefully about which games you really want to get, and try not to see them as cheap and disposable.

More than 10 percent of all electricity produced around the world is used for information and communications technology (ICT).

GAME
OVER

GET A GREEN PET

Don't worry, you don't have to trade your BFF (best furry friend) for a grasshopper, frog, or crocodile.

This is all about taking action to reduce your pet's carbon pawprint. So how big is a carbon pawprint? The answer lies in this equation by a geography professor at UCLA.

Relax, you don't have to do the math . . . the professor has done it for you! He figured out the impact that pet food has on our planet, and

$$F_A = \frac{E^a_{Dog}}{E^a_{Dog} + E^a_{Cat}} \left(P_{Dog,P} \frac{1}{M_{Dog,P}} \Sigma_{Dog,P} F^m_A + P_{Dog,N} \frac{1}{M_{Dog,N}} \Sigma_{Dog,N} F^m_A \right)$$

PLANET-O-METER

the answer is scarier than a giant spider. If the 163 million cats and dogs in the United States were to start a nation of their own, it would be the fifth-biggest meat-eating country in the world! Producing meat puts huge pressure on the planet (see pages 10–14), and their meaty diets give these pets the same carbon footprint as 13.6 million cars.

$$+ \ \frac{E_{Cat}^{a}}{E_{Dog}^{a} + E_{Cat}^{a}} \left(P_{Cat,P} \ \frac{1}{M_{Cat,P}} \ \Sigma \, Cat,P \ F_{A}^{m} + P_{Cat,N} \ \frac{1}{M_{Cat,N}} \ \Sigma \, Cat,N \ F_{A}^{m} \right),$$

Pet dogs and cats are also predators, one of the main threats to wild birds and animals around the world. In the United States, cats capture and kill up to 1.4 billion birds and 22.3 billion mammals every year.

There are lots of awesome things about pets too—they are great company, help get us outside for walks, and teach us to be kind to animals. But pets can't change their eco-impact on their own—so it's up to you to help them. If you already live with a dog or a cat, you can reduce its carbon pawprint by feeding eco-friendly pet foods and avoiding meals and treats made from beef and fish. Keep your dog on a leash when you're outdoors, and install a bell or sonar device on your cat's collar to make it harder for your kitty to hunt wildlife.

If you're thinking about giving a home to a new pet, rodents, fish, and chickens are greener choices. Chickens eat waste fruit and vegetables from your kitchen, converting their energy into eggs you can eat— and are **MUCH** cuter than a compost pile!

Up to 987 million dogs and 752 million cats
are kept as pets around the world.

EAT SLOW

Cutting down on
fast food is a shortcut
to saving the planet.

PLANET-O-METER

Fast food is fast harming the planet in many
ways. It tends to use lots of meat. It often
involves a car trip to buy a single meal. And
each item you order comes in its own packaging,
from cups with straws to tiny plastic tubs
of sauce. One popular fast-food chain has
37,000 restaurants around the world, but
only 10 percent of them do any recycling.

The same company has said it will stop using polystyrene foam containers but has given a deadline that is years in the future. Imagine how popular you'd be if you agreed to clean your room . . . in five years!

If fast-food restaurants aren't prepared to act quickly to save the planet, at least you can. Next time you feel like a treat, try making one of your favorite fast foods at home. It's quick and easy, and science tells us that foods that are good for the planet are also more likely to be good for **YOU**.

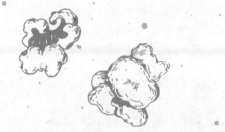

INSTEAD OF GOBBLING NACHOS AT THE MOVIE THEATER . . .

Ask an adult to use scissors to snip a couple of plain wheat tortilla wraps into random pieces. Lay them out on a baking tray and ask your helper to pop them in a moderately hot oven for 10 minutes. Scatter grated cheese, sliced green chilies, and diced tomatoes on top.

INSTEAD OF GOING OUT FOR FRIED CHICKEN . . .

Ask an adult to cut some chicken breasts or thighs into bite-sized chunks. Dip them into a bowl of beaten egg, then a bowl of flour, and then finally a bowl of bread crumbs mixed with salt, pepper, and a sprinkle of paprika if you have it. Ask your helper to place the chicken pieces on a baking sheet and put in a hot oven for 20–25 minutes, until they are golden brown and cooked through. Eat with dips or on a burger bun.

INSTEAD OF GRABBING AN ORDER OF FRIES . . .

Ask an adult to cut a butternut squash or some sweet potatoes into wedges (no need to peel them first—just scrub). Stick them on a baking sheet, drizzle them with a little bit of oil, and sprinkle with salt and pepper. Ask your helper to put them in a hot oven for about 20 minutes, until they're soft, sweet, and super delicious!

INSTEAD OF ORDERING PIZZA . . .

Make your own! It's easy to make a flatbread base—add 3 cups of self-raising flour, 1 cup of water, 2 tablespoons of oil, and a sprinkle of salt to a bowl and mix well with your hands. When you have a soft dough, divide it into four balls. Roll one of the balls into a flat circle (or oval—it doesn't have to be perfect) and add your favorite toppings. Then put it on a baking sheet and ask your adult helper to put it in a hot oven for 10 minutes, until the crust is golden brown. You can keep spare balls of dough in the fridge for a couple of days.

INSTEAD OF BUYING A BAG OF POPCORN
(WHICH IS MOSTLY PACKAGED AIR!) . . .

Pour some corn kernels into a saucepan in a single layer. (It might not look like much, but it will fill the pan with popcorn!) Add 1 teaspoon of sunflower oil and stir. Then ask your helper to put the pan on medium heat with a lid on. Once you start hearing pops, give the pan an occasional shake. When the popping stops, let it cool, sprinkle on a little salt, and start munching.

Snack, candy, and fast-
food packaging makes up about
40 percent of all the world's litter.

SCRUB YOURSELF GREEN

PLANET-O-METER

If you're already taking shorter showers (see page 23),
turn the page to discover how to make them even greener.

Even the smallest choices have an eco-impact—like liquid soap versus bar soap. Liquid soap takes more energy to make and uses more plastic packaging. It also contains a lot of water, making it heavier to transport. Despite dispensers, we tend to use more liquid soap than we need, meaning more waste.

Swap liquid soap and shower gel for bar soap free from palm oil (see page 180) and packaged in paper. To cut down on waste, save the scraps each time you get near the end of a bar. Grate the pieces and add a little warm (not hot) water to make them squishy. Push the mixture into a mold (any flexible plastic packaging will do) and leave for a few days before you pop your new soap out of the mold.

LIQUID SOAP

BAR SOAP

GET RID OF THIS BOOK

Not via the trash can! Remember:

THIS BOOK IS NOT GARBAGE.

It's a book that gives readers the knowledge to make a difference to the local and global environment. Not to mention a really good reason to eat more oven fries. It can't do all that from your shelf. So once you've put each page into action, spread the word by passing this book on.

Pass it to a friend, family member, neighbor, or school library. Pass it to your teacher or principal to enlist help with a project. Pass it to a local politician and ask what they are doing to save the planet.

PLANET-O-METER

BECAUSE IT'S YOUR PLANET, AND IT NEEDS ALL THE FRIENDS IT CAN GET.

INDEX

MORE WAYS TO BE AN ECO-WARRIOR!

ISABEL THOMAS

THIS BOOK WILL (HELP) COOL THE CLIMATE

50 WAYS TO CUT POLLUTION AND PROTECT OUR PLANET!